Unique Geometric Patterns and Optical Illusions to Color

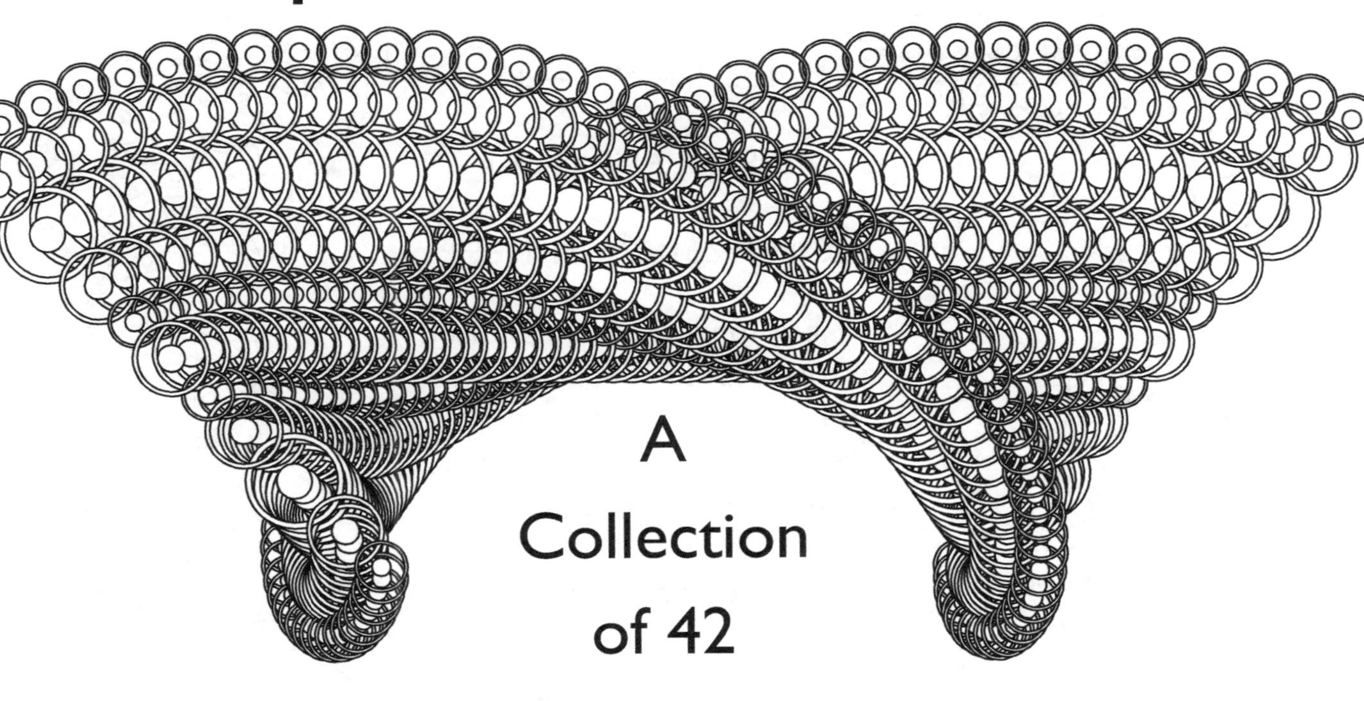

A

Collection

of 42

Increasingly Complex Designs

For Advanced Color Artists

By Dawn McAndrew

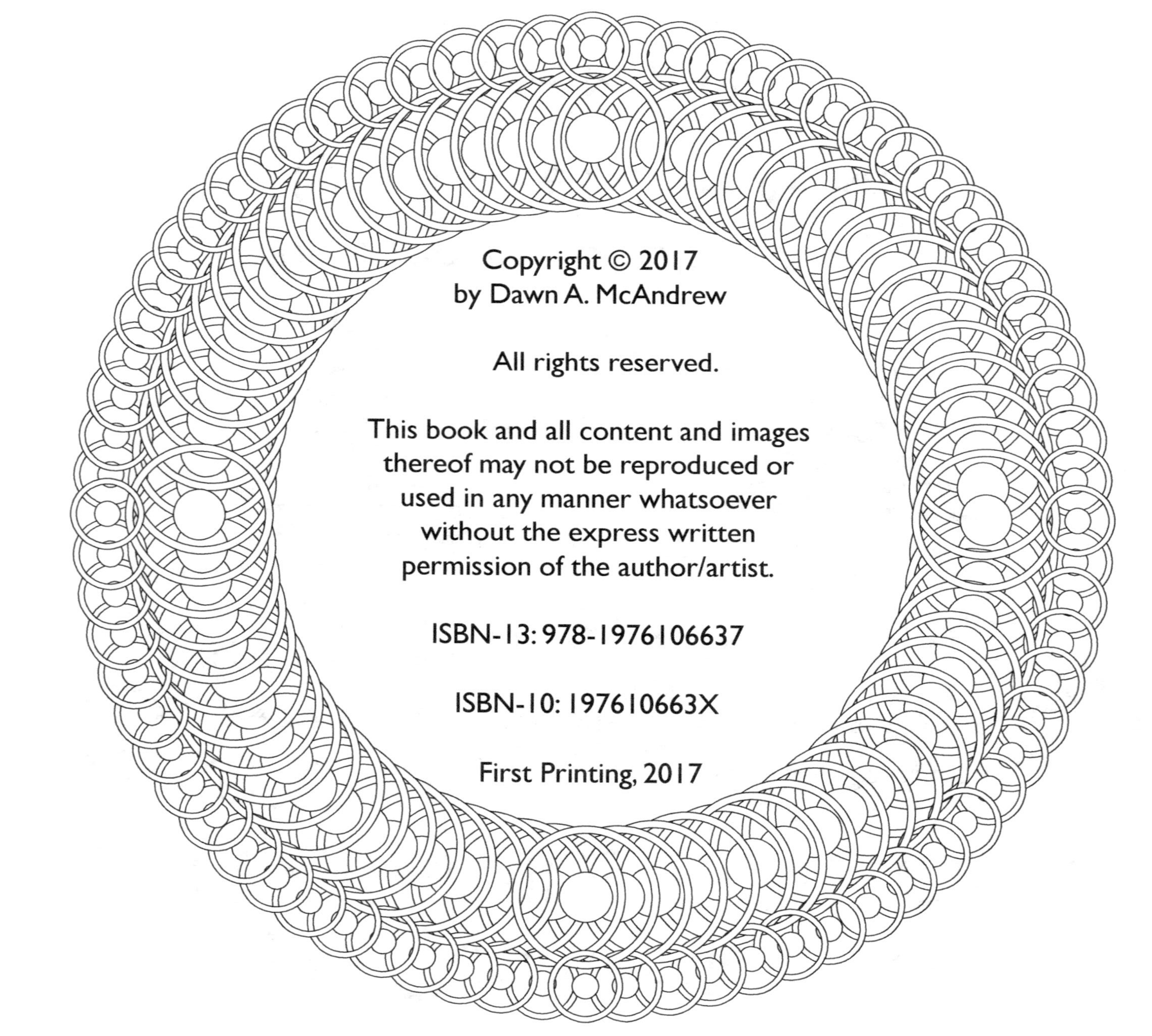

ISBN-13: 978-1976106637

ISBN-10: 197610663X

First Printing, 2017

NOTE FROM THE DESIGNER

First of all, I want to thank you so much for your interest in this collection of unique and unusual designs! As I created and compiled this, it struck me that coloring books are really a very unique form of cooperative art. An artist (such as myself) creates the framework, and then other artists (you!) fill them with colors to complete them, resulting in potentially endless versions of each design. I am so excited to be a part of this artistic collaboration!

So, whether you are the type to jump right in without abandon and color away, or whether you prefer to plan your approach and work methodically, I hope you will have as much enjoyment and satisfaction completing these designs as I did starting them. Oh, and as the approach to coloring can greatly affect the illusory impact of these designs, I've included some tips on the next page to help you get started!

About the Designs

I have loved to draw and doodle ever since I first picked up a pencil as a child. Over the years I've learned to use many types of media to create- pencil, pen, charcoal, clay, paint, beads and metals, words, computers, etc... Imagine my surprise when I was messing around with Microsoft PowerPoint to edit some of my hand-drawn designs and discovered that this unassuming, humdrum office tool (which I had previously used to make relatively bland presentations for work) could be manipulated to create some pretty amazing digital designs.

That's right- all of the designs in this collection were designed with creative experimentation and painstaking editing using only Microsoft Power-Point and its stock shapes and the awesome free graphics-editing software GIMP. I hope you will find the resulting designs as surprising and mesmerizing as I did! And, while this creation was created digitally, the process has me very excited and I can't wait to produce my next collections featuring hand-drawn designs I've worked on over over the years and new ones I've yet to think up!

About the Designer/Artist

I am an artist, a writer, an animal-lover, a gamer, and a bit of a geek as well. I have spent most of my adult life working somewhat "traditional" jobs, trying to make ends meet and always feeling as if something was missing. As much as I tried to ignore my need to create and my need to help better the lives of animals, I finally realized that I only felt truly fulfilled when I found a way to integrate them into my life. Now I am focused on my art, writing, gaming, and spending time with my family when I am not working with animals as a veterinary assistant.

TIPS FOR THIS COLLECTION

1) If you are coloring with markers, place a scrap piece of paper behind the design you are coloring to help prevent color bleed onto the next design. I know, you knew that already!

2) Try to resist the urge to skip to the more complex designs without working on some of the easier ones first. Many of the simpler images in the beginning of this book were created with the same processes/methodology as the more complex ones. This means that once you have identified the patterns and gotten used to coloring the simpler designs, the complex ones should be easier to do.

3) Most images are created using a variation of overlapping layers- identify the primary image/pattern and color the topmost layer first, then the second layer, and so on and so forth. This makes it a bit easier to identify which shapes/spaces go with what. It will make more sense once you start coloring!

4) Once you have identified and colored the primary repeating image/patterns in a design, consider leaving the remaining negative space/background white or try coloring it all one color. This will bring out the 3D illusion better than if the background spaces are colored in various shades.

5) Don't be afraid to experiment with color schemes! Each design can have a variety of surprising and awesome visual effects based on how it is colored. For instance, trying coloring the pattern layers with dark to light or light to dark shades/variations of one color, or even alternate complementary colors. The more you experiment, the more amazing results you will have!

Happy Coloring!

This page was intentionally left blank to prevent potential color transfer to other pages.

CUT ALONG THIS LINE

CUT ALONG THIS LINE

CUT ALONG THIS LINE

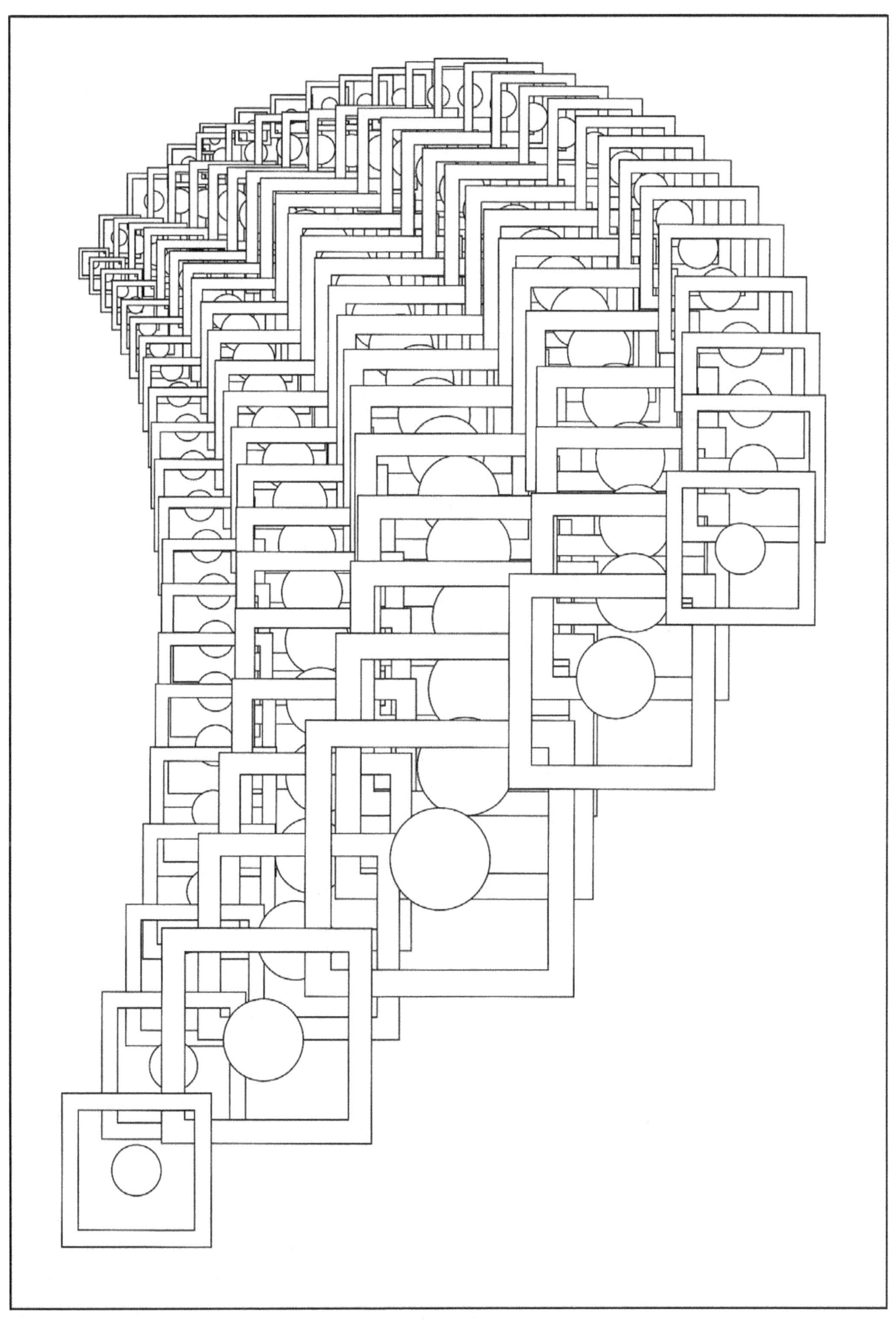

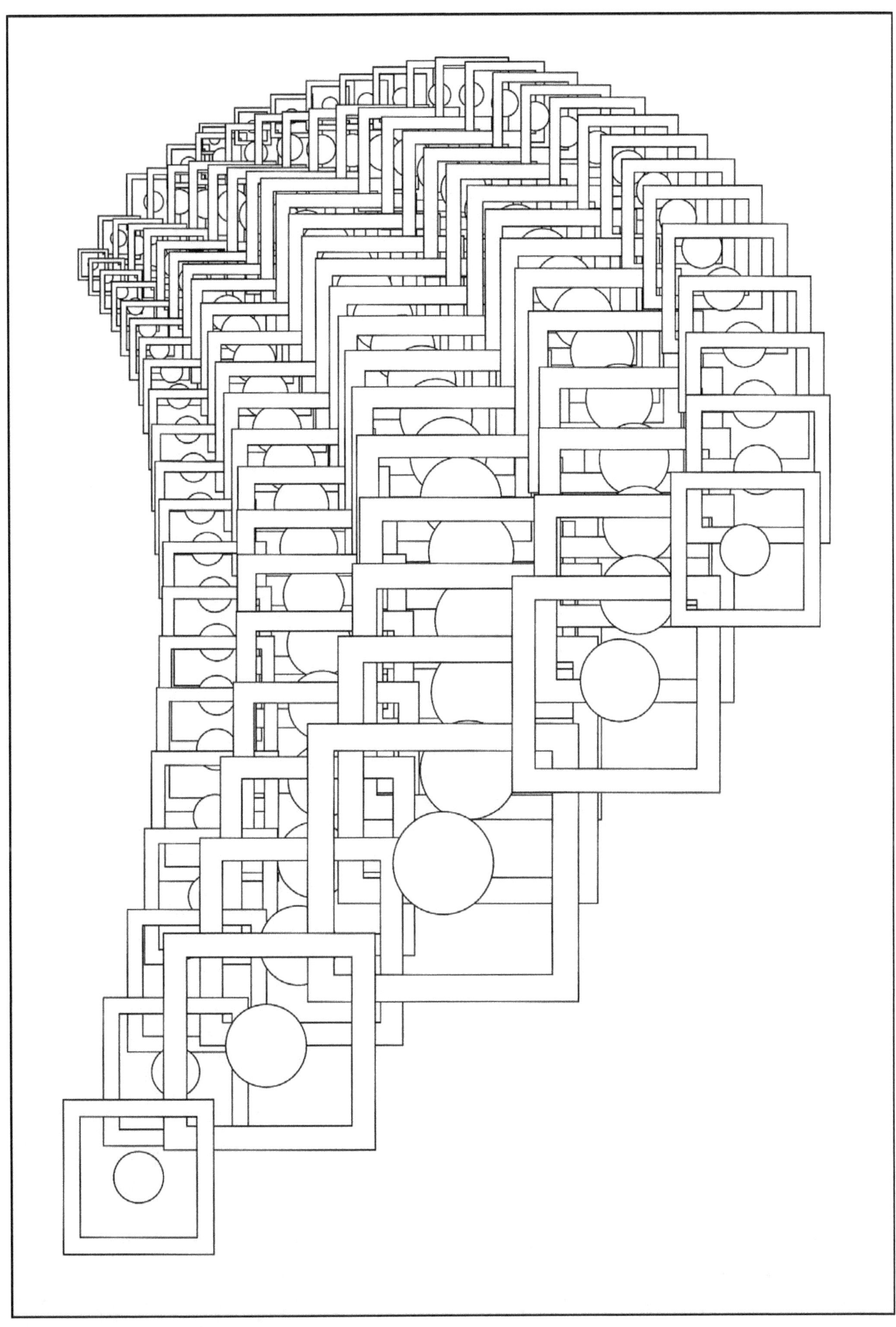

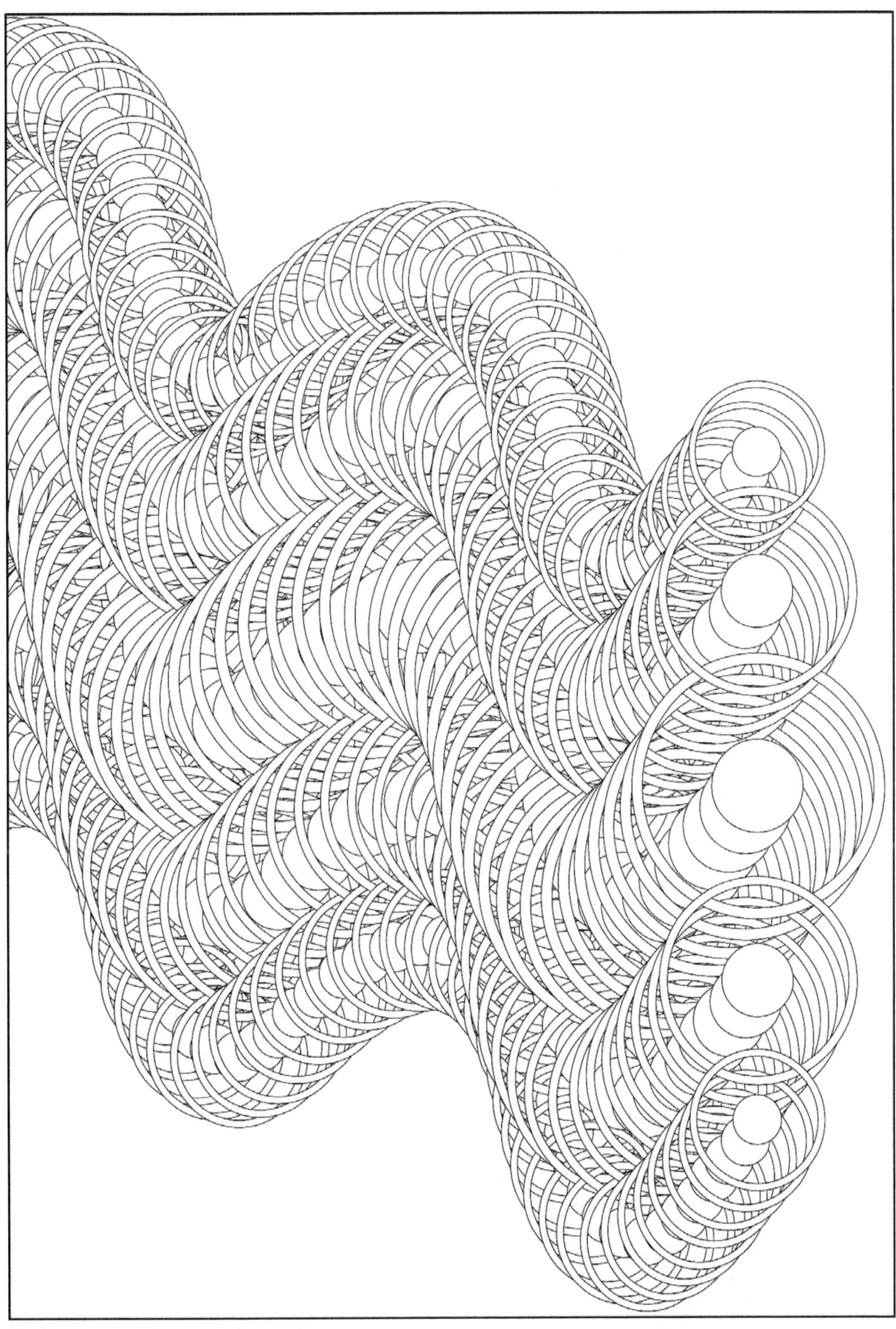

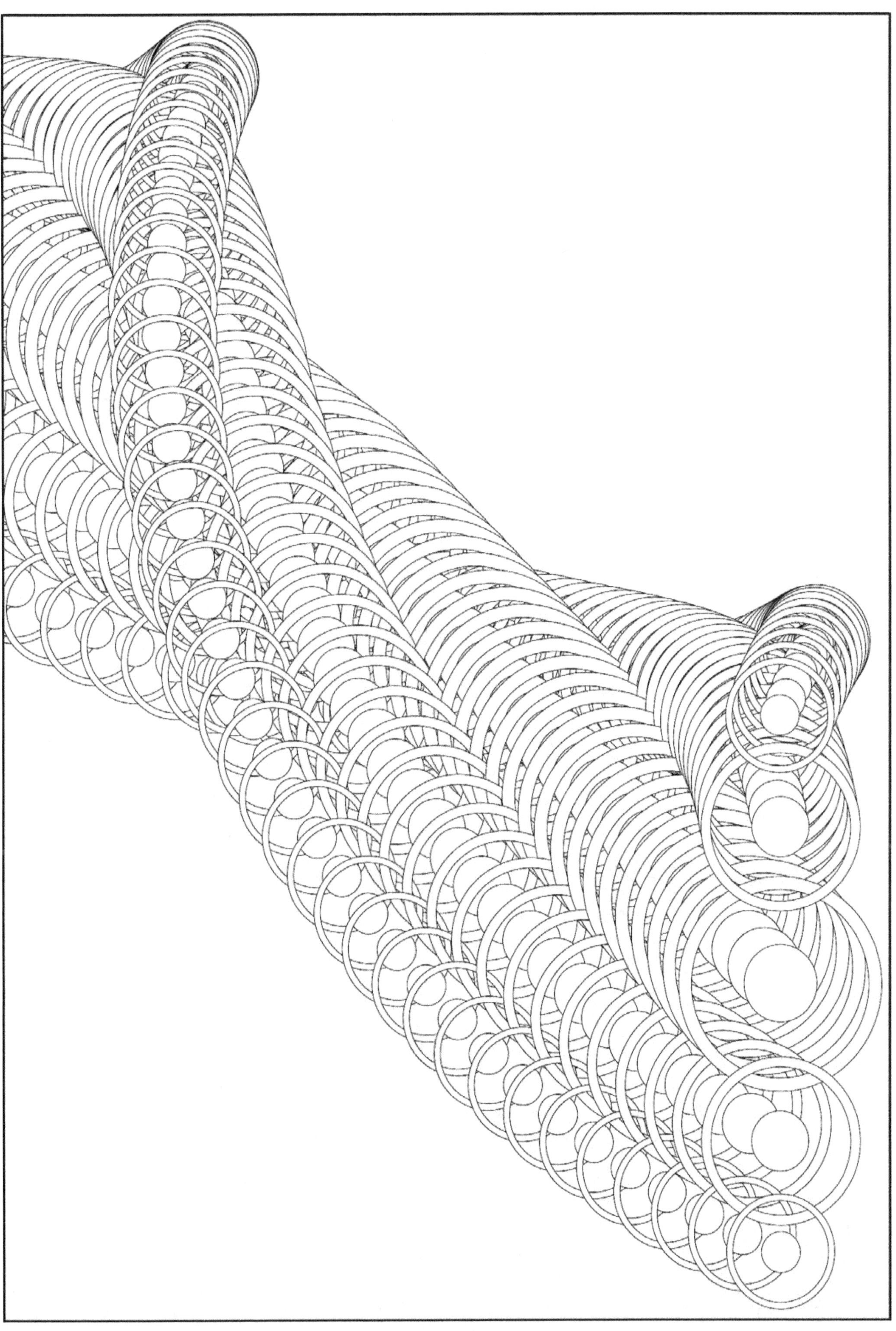

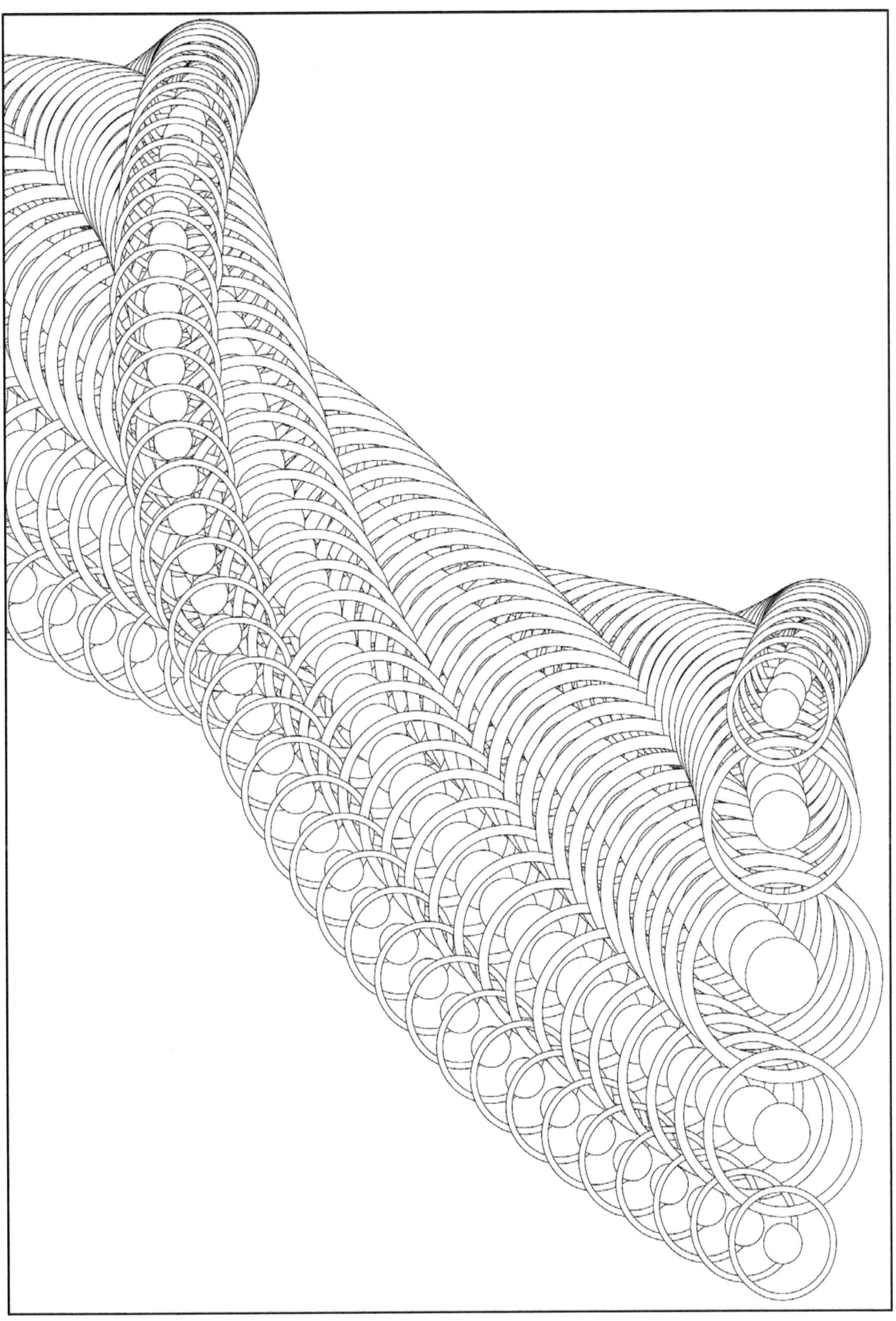

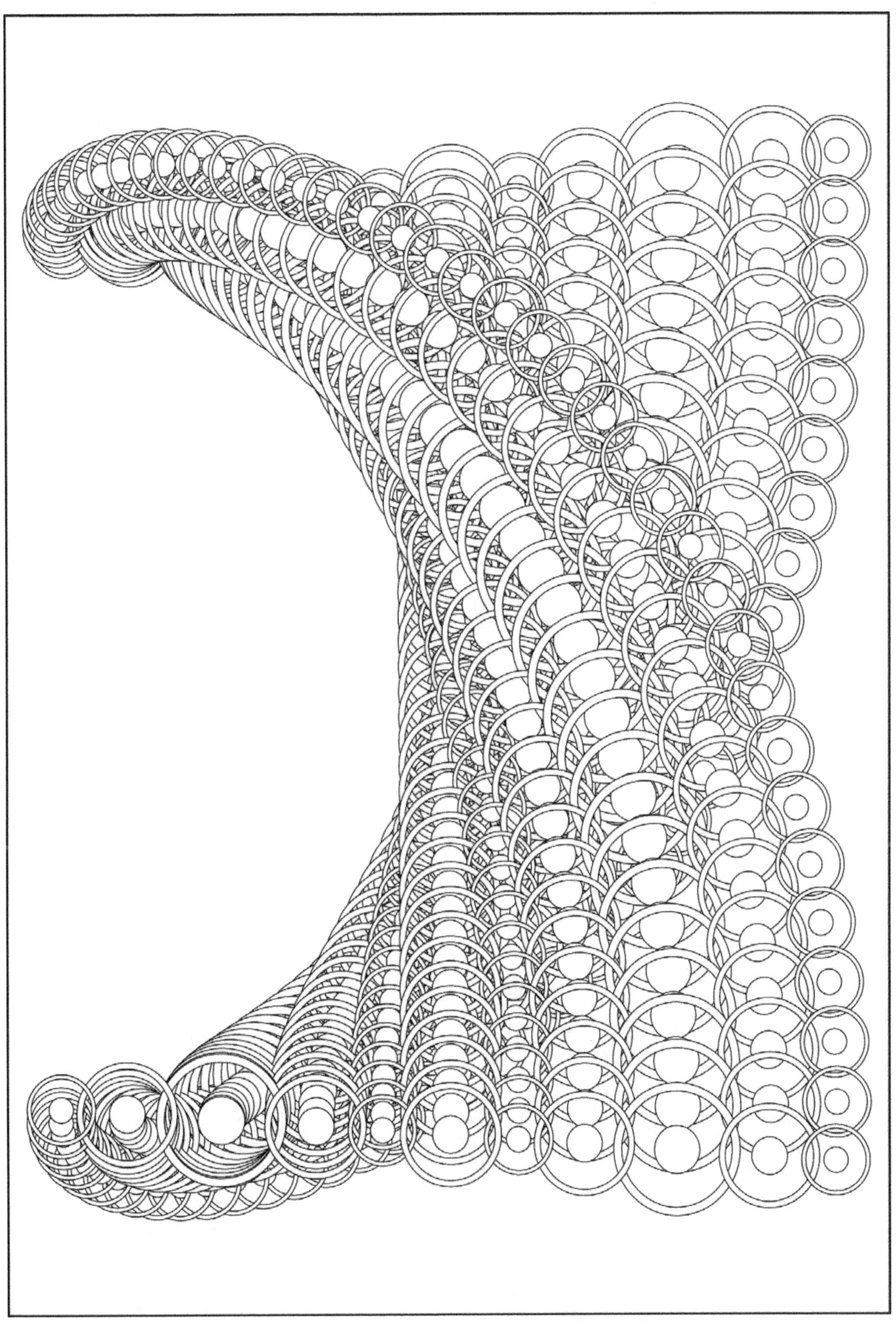

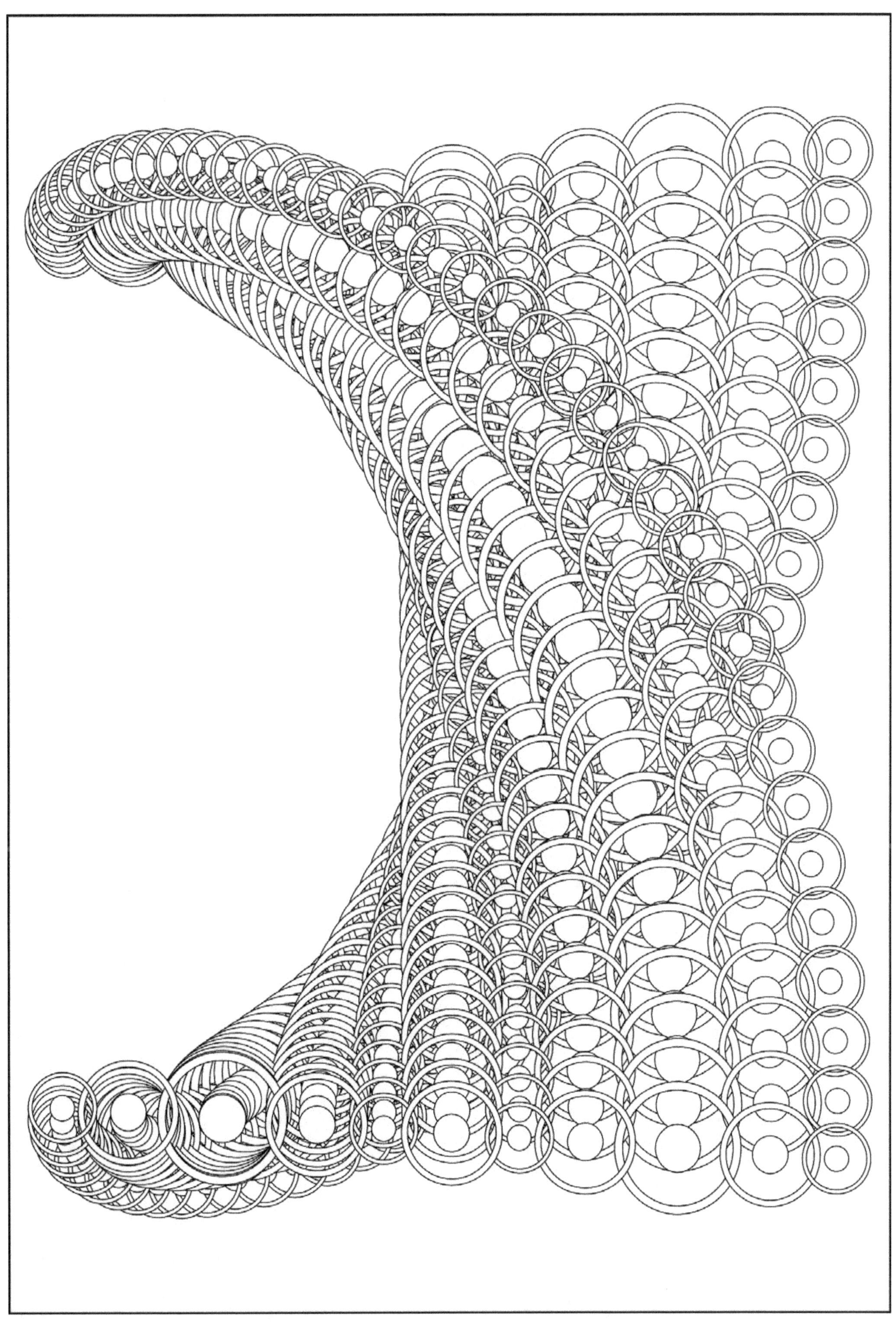

Dear Color Artist,

Thank you so much for giving my collection a chance; I truly hope you enjoyed completing these works of art! Please feel free to share your finished versions either at my website (www.deliriousart.design) or send them via email to: dawn.mcandrew@deliriousart.design !

As this is my first collection of coloring designs and I am always looking to improve, I would really appreciate feedback or a review on Amazon, whether positive or negative.

I am currently hard at work on my next collection, hope to see you soon!

Sincerely,

Dawn McAndrew